WHEN A COMPANY LOSES ITS SOUL

WHEN A COMPANY LOSES ITS SOUL

A Prescription for Transformation

PRICE SCHWENCK

Copyright © 2024 by Price Schwenck.

Library of Congress Control Number:		2024911575
ISBN:	Hardcover	979-8-3694-2364-6
	Softcover	979-8-3694-2362-2
	eBook	979-8-3694-2363-9

Print information available on the last page.

Rev. date: 06/10/2024

To order additional copies of this book, contact:
Xlibris
844-714-8691
www.Xlibris.com
Orders@Xlibris.com
860397

CONTENTS

PREFACE

For nearly fifty years, I have been a humble student and practitioner of management and leadership. While earning my MBA in the early 1970s, I worked as a graduate assistant with a management professor who taught a course titled "The Human Side of Enterprise," modeled after Douglas McGregor's famous book of the same name. Wanting to have some management experience before embarking on a PhD, I took a job upon graduation in textile manufacturing. The tough, command-and-control management style practiced in the mills was exactly the opposite of that taught by McGregor; it proved to be a wonderful laboratory. The three-year experience working in the mills as a line manager significantly increased my understanding and appreciation of the challenges of effective leadership.

The dynamics of management and leadership continued to fascinate me after turning to banking. In the 1990s, I was a regional president at a large bank in Florida. My job was primarily one of integrating and managing the dozens of mergers that took place during a ten-year period. I wanted to improve my leadership skills to more effectively manage thousands of employees working in a constantly changing environment. I was fortunate to find a unique program of study at the

University of Miami based on the management philosophy of Edwards Deming.

In writing *When a Company Loses Its Soul*, I rely on the research and teachings of Douglas McGregor, Alfie Kohn, Stephen Covey, Edwards Deming, Richard Ryan, and Edward Duci, mixed with my work in several organizations.

I am honored to share my experiences and academic study with you.

INTRODUCTION

Today I hear the same complaints from employees that I have heard for decades. "I'm not appreciated." "They don't trust me." "I feel stressed about making quotas that I have little control over." "They are constantly changing what's important." "What does this company really stand for?" "My boss is constantly on my back." "I don't feel comfortable here." "I hate coming to work." Management teams are aware of these types of comments and certainly understand that low morale hinders employee productivity and corporate results. Yet these kinds of employee attitudes persist in many organizations. Why is this so?

The things we do are largely a function of, and dependent upon, the things we believe. For example, when we are around someone we distrust, we likely act differently than when we are with someone we trust completely. Whether or not we are correct about the trustworthiness of the person, we behave based on what we believe. Furthermore, this cause-and-effect relationship between our beliefs and behavior operates largely at a subconscious level. The subconscious mind does not necessarily distinguish truth from fiction; it functions mainly to receive data, file the data away, and retrieve it when needed to make choices. The subconscious mind acts on information that it has stored over time, whether the data is true or not. Complicating matters, the subconscious tends to act as a filter by categorizing new information into already existing beliefs. If the new data does not fit, the subconscious mind may simply reject it.

In organizations, the collective body of conscious and unconscious assumptions, premises, attitudes, and feelings held by management (referred to in this book as management beliefs) and the processes, methods, programs, and techniques used to get things done (referred to in this book as management practices) are linked in this cause-and-effect relationship. Management teams have a real challenge on their hands. The things they decide to do to move their organizations toward desired goals may well be based on incorrect beliefs they hold about human nature in general, and about themselves and their roles as leaders. These incorrect beliefs, in turn, may lead them to adopt practices that just do not work well.

Much of leadership development and training is aimed at improving organizational effectiveness by creating changes at the behavioral level (that is to say, with management practices) and not with the underlying foundation of beliefs. There is no shortage of books, articles, and workshops that prescribe tools and techniques, such as how to effectively work in teams, empower the workforce, delight customers, coach and motivate employees, reengineer processes to achieve higher performance, create dynamic strategic plans, and so on. On the other hand, little attention is given to management theory and the beliefs that exist within organizations. Consequently, it is not unusual for management to constantly change practices in search of improvement, not understanding that underlying beliefs, which have not changed at all, may be the core issue.

A very public example of the consequences of incorrect management practices is the continuing problems at Wells Fargo Bank. In late 2022, the Consumer Financial Protection Bureau fined Wells Fargo $3.7 billion dollars to resolve allegations that it harmed more than 16 million customers who held deposit accounts, auto loans and mortgages. This crisis for Wells Fargo came more than six years after its fake-account scandal burst into public view. Let me quote from a letter-to-the-editor that I wrote in June 2017: "The unintended consequences of top management's use of sales quotas and incentives are now obvious for all to see and talk about. I suspect that CEO Stumpf and his Board of Directors do not understand that the root problem, and their tough leadership challenge, has nothing to do with 5,300 fired dishonest employees but instead everything to do with incorrect beliefs held by top management about leading and motivating people." Since then, Mr. Stumpf and other top executives have lost their jobs, yet the toxic environment continued.

Of course, all companies are not this dysfunctional. I recently did some consulting work for a large regional bank. The CEO writes a weekly email to all 5,000 employees to share what's on his mind. The messages are never things like "We need to make more loans and open more accounts!" Instead, he writes about examples of how people are succeeding in accomplishing the company's mission to love and serve customers and each other. Frequently, he speaks about the company's "golden rule." This bank has won the J.D. Power and Associates' award for best customer service several times and is consistently on the list of the best companies to work for. And the bank is always in the top quartile from a financial performance standpoint.

I don't think I can define the soul of a company any better than pointing out the differences between the cultures of these two banks. Wells Fargo simply has lost its soul.

My aim in writing *When a Company Loses It's Soul* is threefold. First, I will explain what is going on in companies that have lost their way by describing the incorrect management practices, and the underlying incorrect beliefs, that are being used to get things done. The culture and structure in these companies can typically be described as command and control. Second, I will suggest different practices, based on different beliefs, that management teams could implement to significantly increase organizational effectiveness. Third, I will offer ways for individuals working in command-and-control companies to increase their and their team's influence and well-being, even in spite of the limiting environment in which they find themselves.

ONE

Command-and-Control Management Practices

In the Introduction, I define the processes, methods, programs, and techniques used by management to get things done as management practices; and the assumptions, premises, attitudes, and feelings held by management as management beliefs. In this chapter, I will briefly describe five management practices that are used in many companies. In the next chapter, I will identify the underlying beliefs that lead to the adoption of such practices. Simply stated, these five command-and-control practices and their underlying beliefs are incorrect and produce long-term outcomes that are virtually the opposite of those desired.

Ranking

Ranking is the management practice of rewarding top performers and punishing low performers. While on the surface, ranking programs appear straightforward, they actually may be inaccurate and thus be viewed as unfair by those being ranked. Typically, performance in a multifunctional, interdependent organization is a result of many factors in addition to a single person's efforts and skills. A simple equation explains the flaw: $X + Y = Result$, when X is the contribution of the individual and Y is the effect of other factors on performance (think of these as environmental and system influences). The difficulty is that there are two unknowns and just one equation, making it impossible to identify the impact of external factors on individual performance.

Here are two examples of how external factors can impact ranking systems. In a branch bank environment, managers are ranked based on their sales of consumer loans. The top-ranked branch in a city is in a heavily populated blue-collar working neighborhood; the lowest ranked branch is located in an affluent retirement neighborhood. How can such a system come across as fair to the branch managers being ranked? If management attempts to adjust consumer loan goals based on different markets, the ranking system becomes even less credible, as the adjustments cannot be made other than arbitrarily.

The second example involves the impact of different bosses. One salesperson's boss is very micromanagement oriented, requiring several reports and phone calls daily to check on performance and what is currently being done to produce desired results; while another salesperson's boss is in the field with salespeople, coaching and helping to close sales. The first boss wastes the salesperson's time, creates unnecessary stress, and significantly limits the joy and energy that should result from doing one's job. The second boss is a leader who believes it is his or her job to help and build trust.

Incentive Systems

Merit and incentive systems based on ranked performance or contingent requirements (do this and you get that), may be inaccurate and unfair, as just explained. This management practice can create unnecessary internal competition, limit cooperation among employees and departments, and thus lead to sub-optimization of the organization. The win/lose attitude resulting from the use of such incentive systems often comes with the high cost of a work environment in which employees become burned out and frustrated with a judgment system that feels controlling and manipulative.

From a motivational standpoint, this type of reward system may limit an individual by squeezing out self-esteem, dignity, and the innate intrinsic desire to do a good job. Performing work well may become secondary to the rating needed to get the incentive (usually a monetary reward). As a result, the organization will lose the value of the individual's creativity, cooperation, pride, dignity, and satisfaction in performing the work itself.

This critique is not meant to suggest that there are no differences among people in terms of their abilities to produce or that variable pay programs are not appropriate. It merely argues that incentive systems, as described above, are likely to be inaccurate and viewed as unfair by those being ranked. Consequently, these command-and-control types of incentive systems can easily destroy trust between managers and employees and lead to disenfranchised workers. As will be explained in later chapters, the purpose of the incentive program needs to be explored and understood. If the purpose is to control and motivate behavior, there are simply more appropriate and more effective ways to accomplish this.

Management by Objectives

The practice of MBO parcels out company objectives (typically numerically stated) to the various functional components of an organization. The assumption is that if every component accomplishes its goal, then the larger company objective will also be reached. Peter Drucker, the creator of MBO, warns of the potential danger of ignoring the interdependencies that exist within a company. An organization should be viewed as a total system and managed to ensure alignment of all its parts and optimization of the whole.

Those who have experienced the deep silos that exist in centralized organizations know the dysfunctional behavior that can result. Each operating function has its own goals; and for that silo, the goals may make perfect sense; but for the company, they may not.

I'll never forget the frustration I felt as an area president of a large regional bank, when I received a call from the CEO of one of the bank's most profitable corporate customers. He was cosigner on a car loan with his son who was away at college, and his son had missed making a payment on the loan. The bank's collection department, headquartered in another state, was threatening the young college student and treating him like a criminal. His father's company had millions of dollars on deposit with the bank. A short phone call to the father, or to me, would have resolved the problem.

The point is that the collection department was following its rules and procedures by attempting to make its collection goals; unfortunately, the bank lost a multimillion-dollar account over the aggressive treatment of the CEO's son.

Numeric Goals

Often used as a way to manage or control employee behavior, numeric goals, typically tied to monetary incentive plans, are arbitrarily set by management. Numeric goals do not represent action statements for employees, but rather management's wishes for a desired result. The outcome of using numeric goals may appear to be successful, at least in the short run. However, what also may occur is distortion and manipulation of work processes to produce the results required; and even worse, some employees may resort to dishonest behavior to reach their goals, as happened at Wells Fargo Bank.

To emphasize, monetary-based incentive plans (and the numeric goals associated with them) used for the purpose of "motivating" employees is likely to produce unintended outcomes. Variable pay plans used for the purpose of paying employees fairly is quite a different thing. The difference rests upon the beliefs and motives held by management. This controversial subject will be explored in depth in the next three chapters.

Management by Results

This is the management practice of taking immediate action if work results are not those desired. The problem is this type of action is aimed at the outcomes of work processes and not at the root causes of the undesired results. Tampering with work processes in this way often makes things worse. What is needed is appreciation for the variation within work processes and an understanding and attention to improving those processes. This crucial management issue will be discussed in Chapter Six.

Several years ago, I was in a Board of Directors' strategic planning meeting. The CEO of a large community bank had just finished a lengthy presentation outlining more than a dozen strategic objectives, each with several tactics to accomplish the objectives. One of my fellow directors, a former CEO of a Fortune 500 company, looked at the CEO and said, "You know, Jim, the main thing is to keep the main thing the main thing." Up to this point, the community bank had been very successful in differentiating itself from other local banks by giving unmatched customer service; employees were well trained and proud of their relationships with customers. The strategic plan that the CEO presented had no mention of customer satisfaction or the employees who were providing the high level of customer satisfaction. The bank's growth the previous year was below what it had been in recent years and below expectation. The CEO had a limited understanding of why the bank had just finished a down year. His plan was to implement countless new sales initiatives and incentive programs designed to get things back on track.

TWO

Command-and-Control Management Beliefs

The management practices described in Chapter One are problematic; they are built on inaccurate beliefs. This chapter briefly describes two management beliefs that lead to these kinds of practices, which in turn often result in unintended consequences.

In general, command-and-control management relies heavily on the use of authority and extrinsic motivators (rewards and punishments) to direct and motivate employee behavior. Decades of research show that these two forms of control do not produce optimal results in most cases. Examples of undesirable employee behavior are commonplace: indifference to organizational objectives, low levels of performance, resistance to change, low morale, resentment of authority figures, and refusal to accept responsibility. If authority and extrinsic motivators were effective methods of control, these conditions simply would not exist.

Command-and-Control Beliefs about Authority

Command-and-control management practices rest on the premise that authority is an indispensable means of managerial control. Relinquishing authority is seen as losing the power to influence. This is an incorrect belief. There are many forms of influence (which will be discussed in depth in following chapters), each which is likely to be more effective than authority in most situations.

One basic error with the reliance on authority is the failure to recognize dependencies. If there is low dependency in a relationship, there is limited ability to control a person by using authority. With regards to relationships up and down in an organization's hierarchy, not only are subordinates dependent on managers above them for achieving their goals, but managers are dependent as well on those below them for achieving their objectives. The nature and degree of dependency is a critical factor in determining what methods of control are most effective. In today's complex, interdependent companies, command-and-control authoritarian practices simply will not optimize organizational effectiveness.

Another fundamental error with the reliance on authority is the failure to accurately understand human nature. The difference between success and failure, enthusiasm and apathy, even health and sickness, can often be tracked back to an individual's sense of self-determination. Symptoms, such as burnout and stress, often grow from feeling powerless and having no control over one's circumstances. Management must understand that people will resist work environments in which they feel victimized.

Command-and-Control Beliefs about Motivation

In addition to the heavy use of authority, command-and-control management practices typically rely on the use of extrinsic motivators to control behavior. A central command-and-control management belief is that the best way to get employees to do something is to provide monetary rewards when they act in desired ways. "Do this, and you'll get that," has actually become a norm in our culture; it has become a common way to rear children, teach students, and manage employees. This belief about human motivation, especially in organizational settings, is inaccurate and the practices it generates have proven to produce unintended consequences. In reality, the use of rewards benefits the more powerful party, the rewarder, even though rewards are thought of as being in the interest of the rewarded. The use of extrinsic motivators is essentially a form of manipulation and control.

Extrinsic motivators tend to crowd out the more powerful intrinsic reasons (for instance, the joy of learning and doing something well) for a person to do one's best. Research shows when people are repeatedly offered extrinsic motivators, they typically find the task or behavior for which they are rewarded less appealing than before the reward was offered. Intrinsic motivation shrinks, and people are less likely to engage fully in the activity unless offered continuing inducement. Confusingly, as intrinsic motivation declines in the workforce because of the heavy use of extrinsic motivators, management comes to believe they are left with the use of rewards and punishments as their primary motivational tool. However, what appears to be fundamental to human nature (indifference to work, for instance) is actually a result of incorrect management beliefs and the resulting practices.

Observation suggests that extrinsic motivation appears to work; however, it only works in a limited sense. In the short run, managers can get employees to do things by making it worth their while. If people want the reward, they will do the work that is required. Unfortunately, the resulting condition is that the extrinsic motivator often becomes the end, and the work itself becomes the means. The use of extrinsic motivators simply reduces the likelihood that employees will develop an interest in, and commitment to, what they are doing. There is no doubt that people should be paid fairly. The dysfunction comes from pushing money at employees and promising more of it for better performance. While employees may seem to respond to rewards, the very need to keep offering rewards to elicit the same behavior suggests that their long-term effectiveness is weak.

Unintended Consequences

Before presenting more effective practices based on accurate beliefs, I want to emphasize the issue of unintended consequences. In my decades of working in several organizations, I have observed very few instances in which management actually recognized that their actions produced results that were essentially the opposite of what their strategic objectives aimed to accomplish. Problems typically are viewed as the result of poor employee behavior; or worse, problems aren't even recognized at all. To illustrate this latter point, below is a letter that was sent to a bank by a ninety-six-year-old woman. Reported to be true, the bank manager thought the letter was amusing and had it published in the *New York Times*.

To Whom It May Concern,

I am writing to thank you for bouncing my check with which I endeavored to pay my plumber last month. By my calculations, three nanoseconds must have elapsed between his depositing the check and the arrival in my account of the funds needed to honor it. I refer, of course, to the automatic monthly transfer of funds from my savings account, an arrangement which, I admit, has been in place for only thirty-one years. You are to be commended for seizing that brief window of opportunity and debiting my account $30 by way of penalty for the inconvenience caused to your bank.

My thankfulness springs from the manner in which this incident has caused me to rethink my errant financial ways. As a result, it is now obvious that my monthly mortgage payments can no longer be automatic, but instead will arrive at your bank, by check, addressed personally and confidentially to an employee whom you shall nominate.

Please be aware that it is an offense under the Postal Act for any other person to open such an envelope. Find attached an Application Contact Status form which your chosen employee needs to complete. I am sorry it runs to eight pages, but so that I know as much about him or her as your bank knows about me, there is no alternative.

I will issue your employee a PIN number which he/she will need to use in dealings with me. I regret that it cannot be shorter than twenty-eight digits, but, again, I have modeled it on the number of button presses required of me to access my account balance on your phone bank service. As they say, imitation is the sincerest form of flattery.

Thanking you again,
Your Humble Client

The point is that management totally fails in this case to see the negative financial impact (caused by low customer satisfaction and loyalty) of its overdraft policy applied unilaterally without consideration of the total customer relationship.

THREE

Human Motivation

Douglas McGregor critically explored beliefs about human motivation during the 1960s and 1970s. His "Theory X/Theory Y" received much academic praise but not much corporate attention at the time. A significant amount of research has been conducted in the following decades that supports McGregor's early teachings. He presents a clear and basic understanding about human nature that is critical to accurately understanding motivation.

- ➤ The expenditure of physical and mental effort in a work environment is as natural as play or rest.
- ➤ External control is not the only way to get people to put forth effort toward accomplishing organizational goals. People will exercise self-direction and self-control in the service of objectives to which they are committed.
- ➤ The average person learns, under proper conditions, not only to accept but to seek responsibility.
- ➤ The capacity to exercise a relatively high degree of imagination, ingenuity, and creativity in the solution of problems is widely held in the population of the United States.

McGregor arrives at his assumptions about human motivation in part from the work of Abraham Maslow. Some of Maslow's premises are the following:

> Man is a wanting animal. As soon as one need is satisfied, another one appears.

> Human needs are organized roughly in a series of levels—a hierarchy of importance. The lowest level needs are physiological, such as the need for food and shelter. Physiological needs dominate other higher level (psychological) needs, such as the need for love or status, only when the physiological needs are not satisfied.

> A satisfied need is not a strong motivator of behavior. Therefore, when physiological needs, for example, are reasonably satisfied, psychological needs begin to dominate. The key to understanding this is to realize that as a need becomes more and more satisfied, the next higher-level need on the hierarchy begins to dominate. The following describes these needs beginning at the next level above physiological needs.

- *Safety needs.* In a workplace context, the safety need is not a need for job security in the sense of guaranteed employment. It is the need to be treated fairly and equitably. Employees need to believe that they will get a fair deal from management. Management practices, such as setting arbitrary numeric goals, can disrupt the on-the-job satisfaction of the safety need. If employees do not trust management to be fair, this basic psychological need is thwarted, and the resulting employee behaviors likely will not be aligned well with accomplishing the organization's objectives.

- *Social needs.* This is the need for belonging, for acceptance, and for friendship.
- *Ego needs.* This is the need for self-esteem (self-respect and self-confidence) and status (recognition and appreciation).
- *Self-fulfillment needs.* This is the need to realize one's potential and creativity.

In a company environment, if a person's basic need for safety, association, independence, or status is thwarted, that person, in an effort (perhaps subconsciously) to deal with the unmet need, may react in ways that tend to defeat organizational objectives. For example, the employee may become resistant to change, antagonistic, and/or uncooperative. It is critical to understand that this behavior is a consequence of incorrect management practices, not a reflection of one's human nature.

Self-Determination

A more comprehensive understanding of human motivation may be helpful to management teams who wish to maximize their organization's effectiveness, as well as to individuals who find themselves working in controlling environments.

Richard Ryan and Edward Duci have conducted decades of research about motivation, much of which is compiled in a body of work called self-determination theory. Self-determination theory (SDT) categorizes various types of motivation along a continuum from autonomous to controlled. SDT is particularly concerned with how social environments (for instance, corporate cultures) either support or interfere with people's attempts to find satisfaction of their basic psychological needs.

SDT identifies three primary basic human needs: autonomy, competence, and relatedness.

> Autonomy refers to the power an individual has to make choices. Autonomy is not the same as independence, but rather it is having the sense of acting on one's own volition.

> Competence refers to the basic need to feel skillful, useful and effective.

> Relatedness refers to the need to feel socially connected (belonging) by being both accepted (respected) by others and by experiencing oneself as contributing to others.

In general, satisfaction of each of these three psychological needs is facilitated by environmental support for autonomy. Controlling environments can disrupt not only the satisfaction of the need for autonomy but also disrupt the satisfaction of the need for competence and relatedness. In other words, the satisfaction of the need for autonomy allows people to pursue maintaining their important relationships (relatedness) and to develop their skills and sense of doing things that are worthwhile (competence).

Human motivation is either intrinsic or extrinsic. Intrinsic motivated behavior is autonomous, emanating from, and an expression of one's self. People do things because they get significant joy and a sense of fulfillment from the activity. Extrinsic motivated behavior emanates from external sources.

Internalization is the process of a person taking in values, beliefs, or behavior-requirements from external sources and transforming them into one's own. SDT categorizes extrinsic motivation on a continuum, based on the degree to which a person internalizes the external requirements.

External motivated behavior is directly controlled by external forces. No internalization occurs and behavior does not emanate from personal values. People do what they are required to do in order to obtain the reward offered or avoid the punishment threatened.

Introjected motivated behavior occurs when a person has adopted but has not accepted the external controls. Introjection is a form of control that a person enacts upon oneself, feeling that one must do something.

Identified motivated behavior occurs when a person identifies with and accepts the value of the extrinsically required behavior. Involved is a conscious endorsement of the values and required behavior; however, while a person accepts the importance of the required behavior, it does not become part of one's own value system.

Integrated motivated behavior occurs when a person integrates the value of the required behavior with one's own values and beliefs. Thus, this is the most autonomous form of extrinsic motivation.

Some Conclusions

1. The concept of self-determination and the ability to create a way for it to flourish in an organization are at the heart of greater organizational effectiveness.

2. Management's use of extrinsic motivators that fall in the category of external and introjected block an individual's sense of autonomy, competence, and relatedness. This is the main reason command-and-control incentive programs will not produce desired behaviors and in fact typically produce unintended behaviors. Chapter Four takes a closer look at the use of incentive programs.

3. Both intrinsic and integrated motivation produce highly autonomous and self-determined behavior. The difference is that integrated motivation involves doing activities because they are important and congruent with one's goals or values, whereas intrinsic motivation involves doing activities because the activities themselves are inherently interesting and enjoyable.

4. It is common for management to confuse causes and effects. In command-and-control work environments, common management assumptions about human nature typically include beliefs, such as most people must be controlled and directed to get them work, most people do not want to take responsibility and prefer to be told what to do, and most people are motivated only by money. These beliefs may arise from observed behaviors of people on the job. However, rather than those behaviors reflecting human nature, an understanding of human motivation suggests that these types of behaviors may more likely be a result of controlling environments in which

people are not able to satisfy their basic psychological needs for autonomy, competence and relatedness.

5. Integration is an important way for management teams to gain employee commitment to company objectives. While management systems do not directly provide employees with satisfaction of their psychological needs (although many management practices, such as recognition and celebration programs, incorrectly attempt to do so) management teams can create a working environment in which employees are able to seek need satisfaction on their own. Management's job in this regard is to create a working environment in which employees are able to satisfy their basic needs best by accomplishing integrated company goals.

6. An understanding of human motivation can also be helpful to individuals who care to take a proactive approach to improving their level of happiness and well-being. People can regulate their own behaviors in ways that are self-supporting. Chapter Seven explores this notion in depth.

Once these concepts about motivation are understood and embraced by management and employees, the opportunities to improve organizational effectiveness will be significantly enhanced.

This is an experience I had a few years ago as the CEO of a small, multibank holding company. The holding company was a 100 percent owner of five banks, each located in different markets. Typically, an organization's functions are merged after acquisitions. This is done to gain expense efficiencies, which can amount to as much as a reduction of 30 percent of total expenses of the acquired bank. In this company, the banks were intentionally left independent after the acquisition in order to preserve strong local community support, retain excellent top management people, and protect strong revenue streams. My challenge was to devise a way to gain cost savings and, at the same time, retain the benefits of the decentralized organization.

I had been working with the five bank's CEOs for a few years, and we had developed a high level of trust and respect for one another. I initiated a meeting with the six of us for the purpose of exploring the possibility of consolidating some of the redundant backroom functions of the banks. I asked each CEO to give consideration to the positives and negatives of integrating various functions, such as loan operations, deposit operations, payroll, accounts payable, regulatory compliance, etc., into one location. I knew this would be a difficult subject, so I made it clear that nothing would be done without agreement from everyone. From a corporate holding company standpoint, the advantages were lower expenses and better control of the functions; from the individual bank standpoint, the advantages were streamlined local operations in which the CEO and others had more time to spend with customers and business development.

The six of us assembled at midmorning in a central location. I started the meeting by reviewing our consolidated financial situation and presented a pro forma demonstrating the positive financial impact of the consolidations. I then asked each bank CEO to discuss his and her concerns. As I had guessed, the main issue had less to do with the acceptable performance of these backroom functions in a remote location and much more to do with losing control and influence. I told the CEOs that I understood their concerns and wanted us to explore finding a way in which their need for control and the holding company's need for greater efficiencies could be integrated. I was delighted when within a few hours we came up with a detailed, synergistic solution. Briefly stated, we would form a service company to perform these backroom functions; each bank would own 20 percent of the new company and the five bank's CEOs would serve as its Board of Directors. I would serve as the service company's CEO. What an interesting solution; for purposes of these consolidated functions, the five CEOs would be my collective boss! This gave the bank CEOs the true power and influence they needed, and it gave the holding company the cost savings that it desired.

FOUR

Separating Compensation from Work

Management systems that assume compensation is paramount in getting people to work toward accomplishing company objectives are bound to suffer unintended consequences because of the management practices that are adopted to accomplish organizational objectives. Of course, this is not to say that money and "earning a living" to provide for oneself are not critically important in people's lives, but rather to emphasize that compensation programs that use incentives (money rewards) to "motivate" peoples' behaviors are wrought with problems. The objective must be to separate compensation from the issue of motivation.

Problematic Issues with the Use of Monetary Incentives

Based on his extensive research, Alphie Kohn argues against the use of monetary incentives as an effective way to motivate employees in today's modern organizations. Here's a brief summary.

The belief that motivation is a condition and response matter (do this and you get that) does not accurately take into account the complexities of human behavior; for instance, it omits the human characteristic of free will.

If employees feel controlled, research shows that over time the reward will assume a punitive quality even though the reward itself may be positive.

Rewards make it more difficult for managers to establish good working relationships with subordinates. The person handing out the rewards has all the power. This imbalance of power tends to limit trust and open communication; instead, employees may develop mistrust and resentment toward the boss and the work itself.

Rewards put pressure on relationships among peers by creating unnecessary competition. Instead of collaboration and teamwork, what can emerge is stress, mistrust of teammates, and lower job satisfaction.

Managers tend to focus on the numeric goals associated with the reward system instead of striving to understand and improve work processes.

When people are driven by rewards, their focus is typically narrower than when no extrinsic rewards are involved. Their aim becomes the reward and not the work itself. Their objective shifts away from succeeding at and enjoying the task to succeeding in obtaining the reward.

Reward systems imply that people are lazy, will avoid taking risks, and are basically uninterested in work. These beliefs are not accurate reflections of basic human nature. These beliefs confuse causes and effects, which in turn typically lead to increased authoritative practices by management. For example, if it appears that employees are resisting a new program, trust diminishes, and the use of authority and extrinsic motivators appear to be the best way to get things done.

Rewards are usually viewed as controlling. Intrinsic motivation is damaged when people are threatened, watched, evaluated, or forced to compete against others for scarce rewards.

A Practical Way to Address the Issue of Incentives

Ideally, removing compensation from the issue of motivation entails establishing a level of pay that both employer and employee view as fair, and then moving forward with other nonmonetary practices to establish employee commitment to company objectives. Separating compensation and work can be quite challenging because the use of carrots-and-sticks to motivate behavior is very engrained in our society. The main thing to be mindful of is to ensure that the motive behind any compensation plan is to pay people fairly, and not to control employee behavior.

I recently had a consulting experience with the CEO of a community bank located in a large city. The bank had operated during its fifteen-year history without the use of incentive plans, but the CEO was under increasing competitive pressure to do so. We chose an approach that began with a strategy meeting with the three senior executives who managed the bank's ten branches and fourteen commercial lenders.

The CEO began the meeting by stating that he had deeply held concerns about the kind of incentive systems that he had experienced with his former employer but felt that it was now necessary to consider the bank's variable pay options. The three executive officers each related similar reservations based on their jobs with previous employers but also related that their employees frequently asked about the lack of any kind of incentive plan at the bank. We decided to make a list based on our collective experiences of the issues that needed careful attention should we decide to construct some sort of variable pay compensation plan.

(1) Because there are many factors involved in the outcome/result of any process, it is next to impossible to accurately identify and correlate the specific effort of an individual with the process result. Employees know that incentive plans are not typically fair.

(2) There tends to develop an internal competition that usually does not benefit either customers or the company.

(3) Often, the focus of the employee will change from accomplishing important company goals (like customer satisfaction and profitability) to getting a payout under the plan.

(4) Employees are adept at figuring out how to beat an incentive system. The more straightforward and simpler the plan, the better for everyone.

(5) Usually more than one person is responsible for success in accomplishing a desired result. How do we (or do we even try to) account for that? Teamwork can disappear rapidly.

(6) The word *incentive* suggests that the plan will encourage people to work harder. This can come across in a demeaning way to employees.

(7) Another fairness issue is those who are not included in a particular incentive plan can become angry at the company and/or view themselves as less important than those who participate in the plan. In both cases, the system can demotivate important people.

(8) Incentive plans are often changed along the way, especially if payouts get bigger than expected. Trust in management can go out the window pretty quickly.

The following day I met with the CEO, and we made the following determinations:

(1) We would create a temporary one-year plan that would address a single critical need of the company. The bank was experiencing unusually rapid loan growth and was under considerable pressure to increase customer deposits to properly fund that growth.

(2) We would not use the word incentive in the development and rollout of any future plan, but instead, we would refer to it as a profit-sharing program. Fortunately, the mechanics of the plan, and the simple calculations involving the marginal profitability of increased deposits, served to keep the plan design and payouts very clear and straightforward.

(3) We would be open with the plan participants (the ten branch managers and the fourteeb commercial lenders) about the management team's motive—that being, the bank had a temporary problem needing focused attention.

(4) Executive management would share their concerns about typical incentive plans with the plan participants. Additionally, we would stress management's continuing commitment to the bank's existing customer-centered, collaborative culture.

(5) The employee profit-sharing portion would be accumulated in a pool to be paid out equally to all plan participants at the end of the one-year period.

(6) We would communicate to all employees of the bank (most were not going to participate in the deposit growth compensation plan) the purpose of the program and management's desire to learn from the experience, with the aim of discovering new ways of sharing bank profitability with all employees.

The structure and mechanics of the plan and the amount of the payout were secondary in importance to the underlying attitudes and beliefs clearly identified and understood by the management team and shared with all employees. A few months later, an employee survey showed an exceptionally strong commitment to the company's stated vision and values and a high degree of trust of senior management.

FIVE

Building a Culture of Trust

Companies that can build a culture of trust do not need to rely on authority and extrinsic motivators. Simply stated, a high level of organizational effectiveness requires a high level of trust and commitment to shared values.

One of my early management jobs was shift supervisor in the weaving room of a large textile mill in North Carolina. I had never heard of process variation, but I could see it! There were six weavers on my shift; a weaver's job was to keep the set of assigned looms up and running. The looms would automatically stop when there was a yarn breakage. Each weaver was assigned a number of looms depending on what type of cloth was being produced. Production and wages were measured by the number of times the shuttles crossed the front of the looms. It was common to see a weaver with several looms stopped in the off position waiting for him to repair the broken yarn and, at the same time, to see another weaver standing around while all her assigned looms were running. As I learned, this had little to do with the skill of the weavers and everything to do with luck. Years later, I understood that luck was more accurately called process variation; there is certainly a lot of variation in a weaving room due to, for example, imperfections in the materials that are running, the complexity of the weave patterns running on various looms, and the humidity at any given time.

I tried an experiment with the cooperation of two weavers; for a week the two helped each other. No one told them what to do; we made no changes in the piecemeal measurement and pay system, and we did not tell my bosses what we were doing. The results were remarkable; in one week, the production of these two weavers was 20 percent higher than any of the seventy-five other weavers on all three shifts. No doubt, some of the improved production resulted from the energy and satisfaction of working in a team environment (a dynamic that I understood even then to be a strong intrinsic motivator); but it seemed obvious to me that the simple mathematical advantage of having two people working to reduce the length of time looms were stopped was the big contributor. I did not specifically realize it at the time, but the experiment was also about gaining commitment by involving employees in process improvement and trusting them to figure out how best to work together. I could not wait to show the results of the experiment to the plant manager.

The plant manager was furious! He said I had no authority to do what I did; the employees were cheaters of the pay system, and there were no rules outlining how two people could share job responsibilities. These things were true, but what about the 20 percent increased production I wanted to know. I learned from the plant manager that employees could not be trusted to work in teams; it would be too difficult to measure and control individual workers who worked in the teams; the company's engineers had built into the piecemeal system an average stoppage factor so that over time everything balanced out among the weavers; and it was not my job to change work processes, even if well intended. I never did get an answer about the 20 percent increase in production, but I did learn a lot about the plant manager's and company's beliefs about people and how strongly those beliefs influenced the practices that were in place. The two weavers were disappointed with the outcome but not surprised; they had learned long ago that there was no trust between workers and management.

Trust Is the Building Block

Stephen Covey offers a level of thinking based on fundamental principles that leads to a high trust and highly productive culture. *Principle-Centered Leadership* provides a solution to both the control dilemma of how to maintain order yet permit employees to maintain autonomy, and the motivation dilemma of how to gain employee' commitment to company objectives yet insure employees can stay true to their own personal values.

Covey's leadership model is based not on practices (which are situational and subject to constant change) but instead on timeless universal principles—in other words, correct beliefs. Trust is the building block. Instead of relying on the use of authority and extrinsic motivators to control employee behavior, organizational practices are built on trust and commitment to shared values.

Covey teaches that organizational effectiveness operates at four levels: personal, interpersonal, managerial, and organizational. Management teams must work at all four levels, as each level interacts with and influences the other levels. Briefly stated, highly effective leaders accept accountability for (1) demonstrating and fostering personal high character and competence, (2) nurturing high-trust relationships, (3) creating conditions that bring out the best in people, and (4) aligning the organization's strategy, structure, and systems around a compelling shared vision and mission.

From a leadership standpoint, the focus is mainly on underlying principles not on practices. This is essentially the opposite approach of command-and-control managers. In general, individuals honor people whom they respect and trust. Those honored are people of integrity and dependability, of uncompromising honesty and trustworthiness, and true to what is right. Because these kinds of leaders are honorable, others trust them, respect them, are inspired by them, and believe in their goals and visions.

The following four sections summarize each level of effectiveness. Taken together, they present a powerful foundation and practical prescription for creating a corporate culture that promotes a working environment in which people can satisfy their basic needs best by accomplishing organizational objectives. Destructive extrinsic motivators and authority are simply not needed.

Personal Effectiveness

The place to begin is with self, with the individual's paradigms, beliefs, character, motives, and competencies. Covey describes three habits that need to be developed for effectiveness at the personal level.

> *Be proactive*: Proactivity is the power, freedom, and ability to choose responses to whatever happens, based on values. The philosophy of behaviorism (that people really cannot choose their response to stimuli) is simply incorrect. This stimulus-response notion

ignores the human quality of freedom, that given a particular stimulus or condition, people can choose the way in which they respond. When people respond to circumstances based on their values, they gain power and a sense of control.

Proactivity is a way of being, just as is reactivity. The human mind operates as a filter of experiences to produce evidence that tends to support its beliefs. Consequently, reactive people tend to believe they are victimized, and they search for proof to support their beliefs. On the other hand, when people choose to be proactive, they tend to believe the world responds to their value-driven actions, and they too search for proof to support their beliefs.

Management teams must support an environment that encourages proactivity. This kind of environment is a prerequisite for the concept of self-determination, the alternative to authority and the way for creativity and innovation to flourish.

Begin with the end in mind: Practicing this habit creates a mental picture of what is wanted, a definition of a person's roles, goals, and values. At the individual level, a clear sense of mission creates integrity, a condition in which actions are in line with values. In a similar way, a mission statement can give integrity to an organization by defining corporate values and principles. Co-missioning is a practical way to accomplish what was described as integration in Chapter Three.

Co-missioning is a journey that aims to identify common values among all four levels of effectiveness.

Put first things first: This is the habit of personal management, saying no to the unimportant and saying yes to the important, as defined by mission. People need to gain control of time and events to be personally effective. To be successful, individuals need to work proactively on the correct things. This habit can be hugely challenging for employees and management teams who work in companies that routinely manage by results. Many companies constantly change goals or programs for employees. The urgent project of the day tends to make it impossible for workers to determine what is important. "The main thing is to keep the main thing the main thing!"

Interpersonal Effectiveness

Trust is the basis of interpersonal effectiveness. For trust to exist between people each person has to be trustworthy; in other words, each person has to be honest, have integrity, be true to principle, and demonstrate competence. Covey describes three habits that need to be developed for individuals to be interpersonally effective.

Think win-win: Think win-win simply means seeking solutions that allow everyone to win. This mind set is particularly important in organizations where people work in interdependent jobs. The win-lose attitude is extremely strong in the United States. Most people grow up being force ranked (grades in school, for instance) and consequently develop a scarcity mentality. In an organization setting it is problematic to conclude that someone has to lose.

The reality of organizational life is that results are almost always achieved through the cooperative efforts of two or more people. Management teams typically speak in terms of teamwork and cooperation; yet, because they operate from a win-lose foundation, they set up competitive systems (such as ranking) among those who should cooperate to achieve desired results.

Seek first to understand, then to be understood: In interdependent situations, winners and losers and right and wrong points of view are not appropriate. To really understand another person, one first must be willing to be influenced by the other's point of view. Secondly, one must believe that in interdependent situations, third alternatives and shared victories are desirable outcomes. Managers can gain considerable influence and higher commitment from employees if they first fully understand employees' points of view. People are simply much more willing to be influenced, if they feel they are understood and have influence.

Synergize: Synergy occurs when minds stimulate each other and reveal third alternatives. This is different from compromising; instead, it is a joint effort to find a new and better way. Leaders who embrace this thinking value the differences among employees, because they see those differences as opportunities for synergy.

Managerial Effectiveness

The foundation of managerial effectiveness is empowerment. Empowerment is a strategy that creates a higher level of effectiveness by gaining the commitment of employees and focusing their energies on the purpose and goals of the organization. Empowerment is based on trust. Where there is no or low trust, management teams cannot gain workers' commitment; and consequently, management is left with little choice but to resort to authority, extrinsic motivators, and rules to get things done.

Command-and-control is the style of leadership exercised in an atmosphere of mistrust and suspicion; this style creates dependence, conformity, and mediocrity. Abandonment – the opposite of authoritative control – only works if people are independent. Empowerment is neither authoritative control or abandonment nor is it a place in between, but a totally different alternative. The objective is to gain employees' willing consent as partners in a common effort to move them to volunteer their hearts and minds in a cause they themselves have come to share.

Organizational Effectiveness

The critical factor at this level is alignment. Executive management teams are responsible for developing strategies, systems, and structures that contribute to the organization's vision and mission. Remembering that these strategies, systems, and structures are created from fundamental beliefs, management must be careful to view the organization as an interdependent system and understand how changes in one part of the system will affect other parts. Consequently, executive management's job becomes one of aligning and integrating all the organization's resources and components to create total organization integrity. The focus must be on all four levels simultaneously, implementing governing principles at each level. Here is a simple example.

A few years ago, I was asked by the CEO of a large community bank to make recommendations to improve the bank's level of customer complaints coming from the teller function. The bank operated forty branch offices in three contiguous counties. I suspected the root cause of the problem almost immediately upon learning that the tellers in the branches did not report to the branch managers. Instead, the tellers reported to four teller supervisors who in turn reported to a vice president of operations. I learned that this structure was put in place the previous year in order to reduce the number of teller errors arising from tellers incorrectly inputting transaction data. While teller mistakes improved, customer complaints about teller service rose dramatically.

I interviewed several people in the branches along with the teller supervisors and operations manager. It was plain to see that everyone was competent, committed to doing a good job, and genuinely kind to one another. In making my recommendations to the CEO, I discussed these positive observations about the bank's employees and pointed out that the problem was one of structure and alignment. Personal and interpersonal effectiveness was great. Managerial effectiveness could be improved by having the tellers report to branch managers and increase the amount of operations training for them. Organizational effectiveness could be improved by focusing everyone, including back-room operations people, on the bank's strong vision of extraordinary customer service. There was no reason to believe that tellers cannot both give great customer service and at the same time be extremely accurate with the operational aspects of their jobs.

The Power of Trust

Several years ago, I accepted a position with a nationwide bank to serve as regional president in a large metropolitan area. Upon arrival, I engaged in lengthy one-on-one interviews with the senior leadership team (eighteen people) to determine the state of things. I learned there was no common vision nor sense of shared values, and most managers felt at least somewhat victimized by the existing ranking and knee jerk (management-by-results) system that was currently in use. There appeared to be little daily communication among these eighteen managers, and worse, several of them made negative comments to me about other managers.

The performance of the region in terms of growth and profitability was the lowest of all regions across the country. I had recently read Steven Covey's book, *The Seven Habits of Highly Effective People*, and felt the positive ideas presented by Covey would serve as a good foundation for my new team. At one of my early weekly team meetings, I handed out eighteen copies of the book and asked everyone to read the first chapter, so that we could take a few minutes at the beginning of the next meeting to discuss it. At the next meeting, I was totally amazed at the excitement among my teammates as they described what they were getting from the book. Most had read beyond the first chapter and were discussing it amongst themselves. As it turned out, they were also discussing amongst themselves the list of My Expectations of Our Team that we had reviewed at a previous meeting and how these expectations were in sync with the Covey principles. (These team expectations are listed below.)

What happened next was remarkable. This team of managers studied Covey together; we brought in a facilitator from the Covey organization to lead us through the material in a four-day retreat. The team was so profoundly impacted by the teachings that they wanted the members of their teams to also share in the experience. Within the next twelve months, 500 people, from commercial lenders to branch tellers, went through the four-day workshops. In time, fourteen people (only one from the senior management team) became certified Covey instructors. Hundreds of people were writing personal mission statements and personal statements of value and sharing these with one another. The region's mission statement evolved during that year with input from all 500 people. The co-missioning was incredible. Did it make a difference in performance? Two years later the region was the highest performing region in the country. But more important was the sustaining power and creativity of this group to proactively and honestly deal with each other and the daily challenges of the job.

My Expectations of Our Team

Our actions/decisions are guided by shared values (values we will define together).

Our team is held together by trust and respect for one another.

We act and communicate in ways that value all ideas. We say what we have to say with trust and respect for each other and with confidence that what we have to say will be carefully regarded by all teammates.

Our team is highly interdependent and not at all dependent on me—especially as it relates to authority. Control comes from our commitment to each other and to our team.

We see ourselves as part of a cohesive whole—not as isolated pieces. We are collaborative and share information and resources with each other—across our functional structure. We are each selfless; we believe strongly that an individual's success at the team's expense (or at a teammate's expense) is a huge loss for us all.

SIX

Managing Systems and Processes—Leading People

The lack of understanding of the variation that exists in work processes has led to many of the incorrect command-and-control management practices that were discussed in Chapter One. Most management practices are focused only on results; however, it is the method by which results are achieved that is more important. Process variation is an often-misunderstood notion.

Edwards Deming makes a huge contribution to improving organizational effectiveness via his instruction in this area. By no means does he suggest that the result of a process is unimportant. In fact, Deming's statistical orientation compels him to begin with a clear definition of what needs to be accomplished, and then to meticulously measure results for the purpose of continuous improvement. The focus then becomes finding ways to improve the methods that are being used to achieve desired results. This is much different than the command-and-control management approach of setting a desired result and basically using extrinsic motivators and authority in an attempt to achieve it.

The Theory of Variation

The knowledge of variation guides management teams to act wisely in the face of process variation. The output of every process includes common variation, which is inherent in the process itself, and special variation, which is caused by events that are outside of the process.

A conceptual example may clarify common-caused and special-caused variation.

In a manufacturing plant, a machine and a machine operator produce a small part for a larger assembly. The part is designed to be three inches in diameter. Taking actual measurements of one hundred parts reveals that there is some small variation from part to part. Statistically, the average diameter of the 100 parts is 3.001 inches, and the actual diameters of 99 parts range from a low of 2.997 to a high of 3.005 inches. This represents common process variation caused by factors inherent in the process itself; for example, vibrations in the machinery, temperature and humidity differences over time in the factory, and slight imperfections in raw materials. If one part measured 3.100, this is likely to be special variation; investigation might reveal, for instance, that the machine operator accidentally bumped into the machine as this part was being produced. The cause of special variation should be investigated, and corrective action taken if appropriate.

Statistically, process improvement has two components that require action. First, effort is made to reduce the differences in process outcomes. Continuing with the hypothetical example above, the attempt might be to find ways to narrow the range of differences in individual part diameters, perhaps from 2.999 to 3.002. Second, effort is made to move process capability toward desired outcomes. In the example, the attempt is to find ways to produce an average diameter of 3.000.

One of the most typical management errors is to treat common variation as if it were special variation. Not understanding and accurately identifying the cause of variation predictably leads management to create practices that often make things worse. Said a separate way, if something does not go as planned, management may overreact by immediately adjusting ("Management by Results") before knowing the root cause of the deviation.

Management's tampering (defined as reacting to common variation as if it were special variation) has significant negative consequences in managing people. For example, ranking the performance of a group of employees for the purpose of administering rewards is a typical command-and-control management practice. As previously demonstrated, a simple linear equation shows the flaw in this thinking: Performance = X + Y, where X represents the individual's efforts and Y represents the effect on the process of other factors. Y is often a significant factor. Employees must not be held accountable for Y because it is beyond their control or inherent in the work process itself. Instead of ranking employees, management should create ways that common and special process variation are identified and process improvements can be discovered and implemented. The objective becomes not ranking people, which makes no statistical sense, but working to improve process effectiveness.

Dealing Effectively with Process Variation

In the early 1990s, I heard a speech by Roger Milliken, CEO of Milliken, and Company, in which he described a major change that his company was going through to improve the quality of the textile products they were manufacturing. Roger Milliken was clearly the energy behind the huge transformation at Milliken and Company. He spoke extensively and knowledgably about the use of control charts for the purpose of reducing defects. The company's employees were all on straight salary (piecemeal pay systems were outdated) and engaged with management in a continuous improvement effort at the company.

I was working for a large regional bank and studying Deming at the University of Miami at the time; I knew that many manufacturing companies used control charts and wondered if this approach had application in service businesses like banking. Without getting technical, a control chart is the result of recording data points from a process's output and calculating the mean average and standard deviation to determine the variation in the process. The control chart establishes upper and lower limits, which assists in identifying common and special variation. Special variation would be a data point outside of, for instance, two standard deviations. Employees and management know not to make changes in a work process (settings on a machine, for example) in reaction to common variation; they know to quickly investigate the cause of the special variation.

In banking and other service businesses, control charts can effectively be used in operational areas where defects can be measured, for example, data entry jobs. But in service or sales environments, it was not clear to me at the time whether control charts would be useful in understanding and dealing with process variation. I conducted an experiment at large branch in Ft. Lauderdale.

The branch manager was an experienced woman whose branch was part of a group working on implementing a customer-satisfaction improvement project, so she was excited to set up an experiment. We decided to measure the number of new checking accounts that were opened each week and to keep a log of unusual events that occurred during the week. After six weeks, we plotted the date, which showed the weekly average number of new accounts was twenty-seven with a standard deviation of seven. For one week, the number of new accounts dropped to eleven, explained in the log by a key salesperson being out on vacation. We continued this experiment for several more weeks and noted the average number of accounts opened in any one week was about twenty-seven with a standard deviation of about seven.

Several understandings evolved from this experiment. First, the amount of variation in the sales of new accounts from week to week was huge at this branch. From a statistical standpoint, sales normally would be expected to range from thirteen to forty-one new accounts per week. Second, when normal common variation is so large, it is understandable how management could easily react in a low sales week as if there were special variation involved with the week's results and look for changes to be made. Third, while the control chart was of little help in determining either how to reduce variation or increase sales, it was useful in developing an appreciation for the natural wide and unpredictable results in this situation. Fourth, in addition to normal common variation in this process, special variation occurred frequently, which made results even more unpredictable and widely different from period to period.

Control charts may not be useful in many sales and service environments, but the concept and appreciation of variation is important to effective leadership and maximizing an organization's effectiveness. Not understanding and recognizing common and special variation (special variation indicating that there may be a problem requiring immediate attention) within a process can easily cause a manager to make incorrect decisions. In other words, in a work process like selling new accounts in a branch bank, where there is a significant amount of common variation from period to period, managers must be careful not to overreact to a low result believing it to be a special variation. Here is an example of how not understanding process variation can lead a manager to make bad decisions.

I was a new regional president at a large bank. One of the area presidents in the region was having morale problems in his sixteen branches. He asked me to help him determine what was wrong. He and I met with the senior vice president who managed the network of branches. I noticed two things while listening to her speak about the performance of the sixteen branch managers. First, she was critical of the managers' competence and commitment to the bank; and secondly, she used an aggressive daily report card approach to manage them. She showed me data on one of the branches that during the previous year was a top performer in terms of meeting an array of sales goals, but during the previous month was only at 65 percent of goal in those measures. She told me that if the manager of the branch did not get back on track in the next couple of weeks, she would be forced to put him on written warning. She told me the manager was a very experienced guy, a hard worker, and had always been a top performer. She just did not know what had happened to him. She and I decided to visit the branch and meet the manager so I could get a better feel for the situation. We met for less than an hour with the manager and learned that nothing had changed in the previous month to explain the drop in sales. There were no new or different employees, no new competitors in the area of his branch, and no change to his approach in dealing with customers and prospects. He was clearly frustrated by the daily pressure from his boss having to explain to her what he was doing differently to turn things around.

This situation reflected several incorrect management practices that in part stemmed from the lack of understanding that variation exists in all processes, including the process of selling banking services and products at a branch office. The senior vice president was reacting to the branch's latest period's low sales results as if it were special variation. Her way of dealing with the problem was causing unnecessary stress on a branch manager who had a proven record of success, thereby making matters worse. Later, she and the area president wanted to know what I thought about the situation at the branch office we had just visited. My answer surprised them and led to a very interesting discussion about the variation that normally exists in many work processes. My answer was to do nothing.

SEVEN

Personal Leadership

People working in command-and-control managed companies can build personal effectiveness and well-being in spite of limiting organizational practices. The foundational way to do this is to establish personal autonomy and to proactively find opportunities to satisfy important psychological needs.

Stephen Covey tells the story of Viktor Frankl. Frankl was imprisoned in the death camps of Nazi Germany, where he suffered torture and innumerable indignities. Over time, he began to become aware of what he later called the last of the human freedoms, the freedom his Nazi captors could not take away from him. They could control his entire environment; they could do what they wanted to his body, but he could decide within himself how all of that was going to affect him. He became an inspiration to those around him. He helped others find meaning in their suffering and dignity in their prison existence. Between what happened to him and his response to it, was his freedom to choose what that response would be. I introduce this chapter with the Frankl story because it sets an inspiring starting place to work on increasing personal leadership.

Building Personal Power

Understanding the positive correlation between our thoughts and the things we experience is the source of awesome personal power and the ability to influence outcomes in our lives. Simply stated, the thoughts we put into our minds shape the beliefs and attitudes we have about ourselves and others. In turn, our beliefs and attitudes determine how we feel and behave in any given situation. And in the final analysis, it is our behavior that significantly determines the things we experience.

I had my first learning experience about this power at age sixteen. I had just finished football season as a running back in high school. My coach thought it would be good conditioning if I worked out during the off-season with the wrestling team. There was no expectation that I would compete, and I simply enjoyed the tough physical workouts with the team. Unfortunately, about six weeks into the season, the team's starting wrestler in my weight division broke his arm and was sidelined for the year. I was asked to fill in for him in the next match. I agreed but it bothered me terribly—after all, I was very inexperienced, I had no skills whatsoever, I would be humiliated on the mat, and on and on. Sure enough, I lost that match in the first period. Later that day, the wrestling coach wanted to have a word with me. Needless to say, he was pretty unhappy about my performance and focused our conversation on the next few matches that he needed me to be in. After I listed all the negatives about my lack of readiness, he said he was going to work personally with me every day to help prepare me for the next week's match. Among other things during the next several days, he kept telling me how fast and strong I was because of my football and track background. He made sure I knew a few important moves. In short, he hyped me up! The next match went much better—I lost, but by only two points which was very beneficial to the team compared to my dismal performance in my first match. Later, the coach explained to me that the only difference between my two performances was my attitude. In fact, the guy who beat me so badly the week before was wrestling in his first match also. And the guy I almost beat in the second match had placed fourth in the state tournament the previous year. What great learning for any athlete.

We are in control to the degree that we are able to choose our thoughts and consciously act upon them. Here are six directives that have helped me stay reminded of the power of our thoughts.

1. Don't ever criticize, condemn or complain—about others or yourself. This negative low energy is exactly the opposite from the high-energy you need to be in charge of yourself.
2. Care about others and yourself. To do otherwise is destructive and focuses you on things you do not really want.
3. Expect good things to happen. Do you know people who always think the worst is going to happen? Funny how they usually are right, like I was with my wrestling experience.
4. Be enthusiastic about what you are doing, even if you do not feel enthusiastic.
5. Never say or think anything about yourself that you do not want to be true. Instead, see yourself as the powerful, energetic person you want to be.
6. Don't worry. Worry is putting thoughts in your mind about things you really don't want to happen.

Being Mindful

As discussed previously, acting with autonomy and finding opportunities for need satisfaction are not totally a function of one's external situation. We have the inherent capacities to act in the service of our own self-determination and need satisfaction, even despite impeding social conditions within which we might find ourselves. Self-awareness is a foundational element for proactively engaging one's inner and outer worlds. When we become more aware, we become more likely to experience insight and to regulate ourselves more effectively, experiencing more choice, vitality, and volition.

Being mindful means paying attention to the present moment, deliberately and nonjudgmentally, and refusing to dwell on thoughts of the past or the future. This is especially important with regards to negative thoughts about the past (such as regret, guilt, anger, and resentment) or the future (such as worry, anxiety, and dread).

Negative thoughts, and the emotions they create, are formed in the mind. Emotions such as fear, regret, worry and anxiety exist outside of the present. Because the way we feel influences our behavior and experiences, we benefit by being present as these negative emotions pop up, realizing that they and the thoughts behind them are what is causing problems. Being present (conscious) is simply being aware of, and recognizing, our thoughts and emotions. Emotions are just part of being human; and, while that is true, the ability to choose is also a human attribute. We can choose to replace negative emotions by changing the thoughts that are causing the emotions with positive thoughts. Worry, for example, is a negative emotion arising from negative thoughts about the future. Being conscious allows us to be aware that emotion exists in our minds. We eliminate negative emotions by staying present.

We must be careful to avoid putting thoughts and energy on things that we do not want! We bring to ourselves those things we think about. We must understand (and know) that the reason we are not experiencing peace at any precise moment is because we are focusing (thinking) on what is wrong or missing. Instead, we must fill our minds with love, gratitude, forgiveness, and a vision of what we want. Desires, intentions, and passions are merely thoughts. What we intend in our thoughts with passion, we will act upon and ultimately create.

Tending the Garden

I was looking through an old desk file recently and found several pages of reflections that I wrote several years ago about the power of mindfulness and staying present. Those reflections and understandings were especially important to me then. What is frustrating to me is how frequently those powerful notions do not stay top-of-mind. The following analogy is worth thinking about.

The mind is like a garden, and we are the gardener. To ensure that beautiful flowers grow the gardener must water the garden daily (with proactive and positive thoughts), periodically fertilize the soil to keep it renewed (with constant mindfulness) and weed the garden (to control negative external influences that promote reactivity and victimization).

We can stop our minds from controlling us by choosing to replace pessimism (doubts, fears, negative feelings) with high-energy thoughts and feelings of unconditioned love, generosity, forgiveness, respect, peacefulness, and acceptance. What we think about expands.

Avoiding Attachments

One aspect of our subconscious mind controlling us is the tendency to become attached to something or someone. For example, people who must defend their point of view at all costs have identified who they are with their point of view. In other words, self and point of view have merged.

The need to be right, to possess someone, to win at all costs, to be viewed by others as superior, to be accepted, or to be the best makes us dependent on something or someone for the way we feel. Awareness of these types of attachments and the negative impact they have on us is the way to be free of them. If someone who has a point of view different from ours, we can choose to openly listen and try to understand that person's point of view, refrain from judging that person, and drop any attachment to our point of view in the sense that we must defend it at the risk of losing self.

If someone says or does something that hurts our feelings or offends us, we have become attached to what that person thinks or does, instead of being defined by our own values. The way out of this victim situation is to first recognize it and then know that while we have no control over what anyone thinks or says (nor should we have), we do have 100 percent control over how we think, feel and respond to that person. What someone else thinks in no way makes it true. Allowing someone to control how we feel is simply destructive to our well-being. Instead of becoming mad or upset, we can choose to replace those negative emotions with positive thoughts of caring and a desire to understand. Our aim should be to be peaceful and happy, not right, hurt, angry, resentful, or offended.

Holding Accurate Thoughts

Effective personal leadership depends on the thoughts we dwell on. Ensuring the accuracy of those thoughts and beliefs, especially about ourselves, can be difficult. Our sense of self is typically tangled in a history of perceptions, assumptions, beliefs, and emotions that over time may have created a limiting sense of self. To further complicate things, the subconscious mind tends to act as a data screen by categorizing new information into already existing beliefs. If the new data does not fit, the subconscious mind may simply reject it. A personal example may help to explain.

In high school, I was a rather good athlete, helped by the experience that I described in the above Section on Personal Power. At the same time, I was at best an average student. I just didn't think I was very smart. I don't know where that belief came from. As I learned later, it really doesn't matter where self-limiting thoughts come from, what matters is that we become aware of them and that those thoughts are creating our experiences and outcomes. In my senior year, I was uninterested in going to college. Fortunately for me, a school guidance counselor persisted in wanting to know why I didn't want to go to college, especially since my college aptitude scores were so high. That was news to me! With her help, I soon began using the same attitude toward schoolwork as I did on the football field. It made all the difference.

Using Positive Affirmations

A crucial point to keep in mind is this. We don't have to understand the cause or source of self-limiting thoughts and beliefs. We just need to be aware of them and replace them with positive, proactive thoughts. An exercise that many people use to crowd out negativity and self-limiting thoughts/beliefs is to create a list of positive affirmations and review them daily. Positive affirmations are best stated in the first person and reflect things that we want to be true, whether they are true yet or not. Here are a few examples.

I am a compassionate, nonjudgmental, witness of my thoughts, feelings, and emotions.

I am kind to myself and others.

I am self-determined, free from the opinions of others, and free from my past and future.

I am in control of my mind, never allowing negative thoughts or emotions to spoil my day.

I am healthy and strong and full of energy.

I am aware of, and celebrate, the uniqueness of each moment of the day.

I am a talented and valuable person.

I am confident, knowing I am what I believe I am.

EIGHT

Transformation

Many companies experience a gradual downward spiral in terms of organizational effectiveness. When production or sales goals are not met, management blames employees and steps up its use of authority demand and extrinsic motivators to get better results. Employees resist for all the reasons I have described; trust ebbs, resentment builds, and employee turnover increases to an unhealthy rate. Management's frustration increases and pressure for results ramps up even more.

The beliefs and practices presented in this book are certainly not new concepts, and yet meaningful change has not taken place in many companies. What can be done?

Top-Management-Led Transformation

Ideally, transformation begins with top-management's powerful desire, energy and courage to seek a deeper understanding of the cause-and-effect dynamics of the management system for which they are responsible. While each team will have to find its own path, the following six suggestions may be helpful.

(1) There is a strong positive correlation between what we believe and what we do as leaders. Suggestion: Work to understand the beliefs you hold about people and your job as a leader, ensure your beliefs are accurate, and determine whether or not the management practices in place reflect those beliefs. For most of us, this is a tall order, because our beliefs have been formed over a lifetime of experiences. The best way to explore your fundamental beliefs is with your management team. At the same time, this group process accomplishes the important job of developing shared values and trust. It takes courage and honesty for the team to be effective.

(2) Control and motivation are the two central issues with which leaders must deal. This book uses the words *control* and *motivation*, with no connotations intended, to characterize management's main job as it relates to the workforce. Suggestion: Articulate your foundational beliefs about these central issues of control and motivation. Once again, this work is best accomplished with your team. It is important to explore the purposes and motives behind the management practices in place. This knowledge will help the team understand its beliefs and explore the accuracy of those beliefs. For example, the real motive behind a weekly ranking program may be to punish (by embarrassment) and push low-ranking employees to work harder. Continuing the example, once this motive has been identified, it may lead the team to understand that their incorrect foundational belief is that management's job is to ride herd on employees because they will slack off if not tightly controlled.

(3) The many common management practices identified in Chapter One are built on inaccurate beliefs about workers and a lack of knowledge about process variation. These incorrect practices, and the beliefs upon which they are built, are deeply ingrained in most of us and are difficult to change. Suggestion: With your management team and key employees, discover the unintended consequences of these command-and-control management practices. For example, it certainly is not the intention of an incentive system to turn employees into cheaters and to have them focus on beating the system. Yet that is precisely the outcome in many situations.

(4) An important and appropriate management job is to ensure that the organization functions as planned; in other words, that operations are under control. The use of authority to control things has a long history and is deeply ingrained in most of us from early childhood. For example, parents and elementary school teachers often rely primarily on authority to manage children's behavior. However, in modern organizations, command-and-control practices are simply ineffective in achieving optimum results in most cases. The solution is not found on a continuum of more or less authority. Suggestion: Discover more effective methods of controlling things. Study and understand what McGregor means by *integration and self-control* and what Covey means by *co-missioning*.

(5) The use of extrinsic motivators, such as monetary incentives, tied to the accomplishment of a goal or a task, is commonplace in our society. The practice of using rewards and punishments appears to work; however, this practice only works in a limited way. People will normally attempt to achieve desired rewards or avoid punishments; but at the same time, attitudes about work typically

change in a negative way; the intrinsic pleasure of accomplishing a task or meeting an important goal wane, and a feeling of being manipulated forces out feelings of trust and fairness. All of these have a huge cost to the organization. Suggestion: Find ways to gain employee commitment to achieving company objectives. Study and understand self-determination theory and what Deming means by creating an environment in which people can find joy and pride in their work.

(6) When the top-management team understands clearly where it wants to go, it needs to build an implementation plan to transform the entire organization. Suggestion: Pass the knowledge learned in the first five steps to key groups of line supervisors and employees and have them share in the development of an implementation plan.

Vision

The Board of Directors and the Executive Management Team are responsible for their organization's long-term success and survival. Their overriding aim must be to optimize the interests of all the organization's inter-dependent stakeholders, including stockholders, customers, employees, and communities. Three points are crucial to a full understanding of the wisdom of this vision.

First, long-term vision requires a shared and compelling mission that inspires all stakeholders and always remains the main thing. When, for example, this quarter's profit or today's stock price becomes the priority, the board's and management's short-term decisions and tactics can seriously damage their organization's well-being and even its survival.

Second, *optimizing* the interests of all stakeholders suggests something much more complex than *maximizing* the interests of the organization's stakeholders. If the board and management, for example, are focused primarily on maximizing their company's short-term profits, customers and employees are likely to be negatively impacted by the strategies that are being used. Finding the right balance and incorporating that into management's decision-making is a critical challenge, requiring unwavering commitment to the company's vision.

Third, *inter-dependent* stresses the reality of the importance of all stakeholders working in concert for the long-term well-being and effectiveness of the organization. When management uses command-and-control practices to get things done, for example, the organization is bound to suffer for the reasons discussed in previous chapters.

An interesting thing to ponder is the use of *authority* in the military. *Orders* are to be carried out without question. While this is certainly the case, it is also obvious that there exists an extremely powerful vision. Perhaps the shared commitment to a compelling vision (and not authority) is the overriding factor to the military's strong organizational effectiveness.

Division- or Department-Led Transformation

In Chapter Five under the heading "The Power of Trust," I described an experience I had as a regional president of a large company. The transformation of our group was amazing. Nothing we did required the approval of top management; we simply decided to join together around shared values to improve our work experience. We studied together, we learned together, and we changed together. There were obviously many corporate-level things, such as the command-and-control incentive system, we could not change, but we worked to understand the dynamics of what was going on and why. Importantly, the mutual learning about things, such as process variation and self-determination theory, provided useful tools to increase the effectiveness of our group.

People have considerable influence when they join based on shared values, when they come together to learn and achieve worthwhile things, and when they celebrate each other. If this can be accomplished, it fulfills the basic psychological needs we have as human beings, and thus nourishes the well-being and the soul of the group. So in and of itself, it is a worthwhile endeavor. And in the final analysis, there is not a more effective way to influence top management than by group excellence.

Some Final Thoughts

In the past couple of years, much has been said about young people moving into the workplace; in turn, these young people have had much to say about what they claim is an outdated workplace. In an early-2024 survey, a majority of business owners reported that their younger employees were the least reliable of all their workers and the most likely to create division and toxicity. Most employers feel that this newest generation of workers (referred to as Generation Z) act entitled and do not fit their company cultures. At the same time, surveys show that many young people see hierarchical structures as rigid, limiting creativity, and unfair to workers.

Let's look at this new generation of people moving into the workplace. With the aim of this book in mind, let us examine whether the understandings and practices prescribed are applicable to both employer and employee.

The Generation Z population (people born from 1997 to 2012) will comprise nearly 25 percent of the workforce by the end of 2024. And this group will grow significantly as the younger Gen-Zers (still in high school and college today) enter the workforce for the first time and older workers retire. Today (2024), Generation Z makes up about 20 percent of the United States population. It is the most diverse generation: 51 percent White, 25 percent Hispanic, 14 percent Black, and 6 percent Asian.

Because of the size and makeup of the Gen Z population, management's challenge is to determine how to deal with this group in order to optimize organization effectiveness. And, too, the challenge for Gen-Zers is to find ways to effectively integrate and influence the organization's beliefs and practices.

Generation Z Priorities about Work

Gen-Zers tend to prefer career options centered on flexibility and autonomy. One study found that 60 percent of Gen-Zers describe typical nine-to-five jobs as "soul-sucking." This is why many young people are rejecting the traditional nine-to-five schedule in favor of remote work options that offer more flexibility and a greater sense of work-life balance.

Surveys show a majority of Gen-Zers care about social change, racial equity, and protecting the environment. They value corporate social responsibility and work-life blend. They are driven to make a difference and seek employment with organizations that share similar values as their own. They seek trust and support in a manager above any other managerial quality.

Gen-Zers have grown up with the ability to share their thoughts publicly and receive real-time feedback through social media. As a result, they expect their ideas to be heard and respected in the workplace. They prioritize authenticity, truth, and connectivity in their relationships.

Of course, there is much variation in terms of priorities among the Generation Z population. However, the following compilation of the answers to three questions asked of a number of college seniors in early 2024 offers an interesting perspective of an important subset of the group. (1) What are your most important priorities about work life? (2) What workplace norms do you reject? (3) What are the most important cultural criteria you look for in a prospective employer?

1. As a Gen Z entering the workforce, my most important priorities about work life revolve around several key factors. Firstly, I prioritize a healthy work-life balance, recognizing the importance of both personal and professional fulfillment. Secondly, I seek opportunities for continuous learning and growth, whether through training programs or mentorship. Third, I value a supportive and inclusive work environment where diversity is celebrated, and everyone feels respected and valued. Lastly, I prioritize a workplace that aligns with my own values to intentionally foster a sense of fulfillment, motivation, and overall satisfaction within a job. By this, I mean that I have been looking for a company whose mission, culture, and practices resonate with what I personally believe in.

2. In today's dynamic work environment, I reject workplace norms that prioritize quantity of work over the quality of work, advocating for a results-oriented approach where productivity is measured by output rather than hours worked. I also reject strict hierarchical structures that limit creativity and teamwork, favoring more collaborative and inclusive leadership styles that empower employees at all levels to contribute and make decisions.

3. When evaluating prospective employers, there are certain key criteria I look for. First, I value transparency and open communication, seeking employers who are honest and forthcoming about their goals, challenges, and successes. I also prioritize companies that encourage employees to take risks, experiment, and think creatively, while providing constructive feedback rather than punitive measures. Lastly, I seek companies that are committed to social and environmental responsibility, demonstrating a genuine concern for the well-being of society and the planet.

Certainly, there are differences among the generations in terms of their priorities resulting from world events and changing political and cultural attitudes of their times. But in terms of basic human needs and desires, is there really a significant difference between this younger group of workers and other generations of employees? I do not believe so.

Generation Z in a Transformed Organization

Embracing the prescriptions presented in this book, a company can deal quite effectively with this new generation of employees. Also, I believe Gen-Zers can benefit from having a clear understanding of the organizational and psychological dynamics at play, as well as developing their personal leadership (as described in Chapter Seven). Here are a few closing comments.

1. Companies that depend on authority and extrinsic motivators may certainly have more difficulty managing Gen-Zers than other generations. However, as presented in previous chapters, these command-and-control practices will not produce optimal results and typically cause serious unintended consequences. This is the case regardless of the age of the employee.

2. Chapters Three and Four look deeply into the issue of human motivation. As discussed, management practices that support the satisfaction of employees' psychological needs simply yield more effective organizations. Survey results reveal that Gen-Zers' need flexibility and autonomy; work that makes a difference (in other words, the job must be more than about money); a mutually respectful work environment; an opportunity for continuous learning and growth; and supportive management structures that promote creativity and teamwork. These needs and desires are no different from those expressed in decades of research regarding all employee needs and desires.

3. Gen-Zers seek trust and support in a manager above any other managerial quality. They seek employment with companies whose values align with their own. Chapter Five emphasizes the importance of a high level of trust and commitment to shared values. Transformed companies simply do not need to rely on command-and-control practices to manage people.

4. Many Gen-Zers (and others as well) express a desire for remote work. At the same time, they express a need for teamwork, respect for others, and an inclusive work environment where diversity is

celebrated, and everyone feels valued. Interestingly, these needs usually are met best with face-to-face contact. Surely, both employer and employee can find new ways to accommodate a healthy work-life balance and provide desirable interpersonal relationships that support the need for Relatedness.

5. Lastly, Gen-Zers want to work for companies that prioritize quality of work, corporate citizenship, inclusion in the workforce, and fairness. These are obviously qualities of companies with soul.

In the Final Analysis

Transformation from a command-and-control management system to an enlightened leadership model with soul will be a major undertaking. But with the rapidly changing and divisive world in which we live today, it is more important than ever for companies to take the challenge. While it may take considerable effort and time to fully transform to a new culture, the work to get there will dramatically change the heart and soul of the company and everyone associated with it.

9 798369 423646